At dawn on December 2, 1805, a cold mist hung over the fields near Austerlitz in the Austrian Empire. More than 150,000 soldiers fought for their lives in the dim light. Napoleon, emperor of France, paced his horse on a hill overlooking the scene

Fatal Mistake

Pulling his horse to a halt, Napoleon saw enemy soldiers on the move below. They were deserting the center of their line to attack his right flank. *Stupid fools*, Napoleon thought. *Never weaken your center*. He gave the order to attack.

One Sharp Blow

In a few hours it was over. With one swift charge, the French army broke through the enemy line. It crushed the Austrian and Russian armies. At least 15,000 soldiers lay dead on the battlefield. Now all of Europe was within Napoleon's grasp.

Blood-Soaked Glory

Napoleon accepted the surrenders of the Austrian and Russian emperors. Then he walked the battlefield, stepping over corpses. "This," he told an aide, "is the

The Question

How was Napoleon able to make himself emperor when the French people had just fought so hard to get rid of their king? Why is it difficult for one person to hold on to vast amounts of power?

PREVIEW PHOTOS

PAGE 1: Napoleon looks over his troops during a reenactment of the Battle of Austerlitz in 2007.

PAGES 2–3: French troops (in blue) battle Russian cavalrymen during the Battle of Austerlitz.

PAGES 4–5: Napoleon (on white horse) gives orders at Austerlitz.

Book Design: Red Herring Design/NYC **Photo Credits:** Photographs © 2012: Alamy Images/The Art Gallery Collection: 44 top right; Art Resource, NY: 21 (Joseph Pierre Bazin/Scala/White Images), 24 (Jacques Louis David/Erich Lessing), 16 (Antoine Jean Gros/Erich Lessing), 34 (Johann Adam Klein/Musée de l'Armée/Dist. Réunion des Musées Nationaux), 45 bottom right (Jean Baptiste Mauzaisse/Réunion des Musées Nationaux/Daniel Arnaudet/Gérard Blot), 45 bottom left (Ernest Meissonier/Erich Lessing), 33 (Knud Petersen/Kunstbibliothek, Staatliche Museen, Berlin/Bildarchiv Preussischer Kulturbesitz), 44 top left (Felix Philippoteaux/Réunion des Musées Nationaux), 45 top right (Olivier Pichat/Réunion des Musées Nationaux/Gérard Blot), 40 (Oscar Rex/Chateaux de Malmaison et Bois-Preau, Rueil-Malmaison, France/Réunion des Musées Nationaux); Bridgeman Art Library International Ltd., London/New York: 13 (Bibliotheque Nationale, Paris/Archives Charmet), 29 center top (Michel-Martin Drolling/Private Collection/© Rafael Valls Gallery, London), 29 center bottom (Joseph Franque/Bibliotheque Marmottan, Boulogne-Billancourt, Paris/Giraudon), 15 top (Jean-Jacques Hauer/Musee de la Ville de Paris, Musee Carnavalet, Paris/Giraudon), 36 (Francois Joseph Heim/Musée de l'Armée, Brussels/Patrick Lorette/Giraudon), 39 (Robert Alexander Hillingford/Private Collection/© Bonhams, London), 14 right (Louvre, Paris/Peter Willi), 15 bottom (Musee de la Ville de Paris, Musee Carnavalet, Paris/Giraudon), 41 (Private Collection/© Agnew's, London), 29 top right (Sebastian Weygandt/Neue Galerie, Kassel, Germany/© Museumslandschaft Hessen Kassel/Ute Brunzel), 29 top left (Jean Baptiste Joseph Wicar/Galleria d'Arte Moderna, Palazzo Pitti, Florence/Alinari); Courtesy of Donald A. Heald Gallery: 29 bottom left; Getty Images: 8, 28 top (Jacques Louis David/The Bridgeman Art Library), 10 (Universal History Archive); Mark Summers: cover; NEWSCOM: 14 background, 18, 26, 29 bottom right, 45 top center (akg-images), 29 center (Lauren Lecat/akg-images), 1 (Otto Ballon Mierny/AFP/Getty Images), 43 (Karl von Steuben/akg-images), 2, 3 (Bogdan Pawlowitsch Willewalde/akg-images); ShutterStock, Inc.: 14 left (agorulko), back cover (Michael Drager), 44 center (Magcom); Superstock, Inc.: 42 (Andrea Appiani I/Kunsthistorisches Museum, Vienna), 30 (Paul Delaroche/Musee de L'Armee, Paris), 22 (Jean Auguste Dominique Ingres/Musee de L'Armee, Paris), 44 top center, 45 top left (Lefevre/Réunion des Musées Nationaux), 28 bottom, 29 bottom center (The Art Archive); The Granger Collection, New York/Rue des Archives: 44 bottom left; The Image Works: 44 bottom right (State Borodino War and History Museum, Moscow/Fine Art Images/Heritage Images), 4, 5 (Carle Vernet/Museum of Versailles/Roger-Viollet).

Maps by David Lindroth, Inc.

Library of Congress Cataloging-in-Publication Data
Baicker, Karen.
Napoleon complex : a young general takes France by storm / Karen Baicker.
p. cm. — (Xbooks)
Includes bibliographical references and index.
ISBN-13: 978-0-545-32938-5
ISBN-10: 0-545-32938-8
1. Napoleon I, Emperor of the French, 1769-1821—Juvenile literature.
I. Title.
DC203.B14 2012
944.05092—dc23
[B]
2011032087

NAPOLEON COMPLEX

A Young General Takes
France by Storm

KAREN BAICKER

NAPOLEON LEADS HIS MEN over the Alps in this famous painting by Jacques-Louis David.

TABLE OF CONTENTS

1

Hero's Welcome

Napoleon returns from battle
and conquers his own country.

In the fall of 1799, General Napoleon Bonaparte
arrived in France to wild cheering. He had spent the last
14 months trying to conquer Egypt. And the French
people greeted him as though he had succeeded.
Cannon fire boomed in Paris. Bands paraded through
the streets.

In reality, the 30-year-old general's campaign in
Egypt had been a miserable failure. But at the moment,

that didn't matter. The French people needed a hero, and Napoleon was certain he was the man.

France had been in turmoil for years. In 1789 the French had launched a revolution against their government. Within a few years they beheaded their king and queen. They turned France into a republic—a country ruled by elected leaders. "Liberty, equality, and brotherhood" was the revolutionaries' rallying cry.

Reign of Terror

But the lofty goals of the revolution were soon drowned in violence. Enemies at home and abroad kept France in a constant state of war. And the new leaders in Paris turned out to be as brutal as any king.

France was on the brink of disaster, and Napoleon seemed like a savior. The cocky young general instilled discipline in his soldiers. He got things done.

On November 10, Napoleon decided the time was right to seize power. Surrounded by his officers, he burst into the legislature and announced that he had arrived to save the republic.

The reaction wasn't what Napoleon had hoped it

LEGISLATORS ATTACK Napoleon with daggers.

would be. Angry legislators attacked Napoleon until a group of his followers hustled him out of the room.

Napoleon's soldiers stormed the building with their bayonets drawn. Terrified lawmakers fled through the windows. That night, three consuls were chosen to rule France. The First Consul would be Napoleon.

Napoleon promised to protect the ideals of the revolution. But he hinted that democracy would not be part of the deal. "The Revolution is over," he proclaimed. "I am the Revolution."

Off with Their Heads!

Here are five things you should know about the revolutionaries who beheaded their king.

1 THEY WERE GROUNDBREAKERS.
Kings and queens had been overthrown before—but only to make way for other monarchs. Rebels in the United States had just won independence from the British monarchy. But the French were the first to completely get rid of a homegrown monarchy.

2 THEY WERE HUNGRY.
The French revolutionaries fought for "liberty, equality, and brotherhood." But they also fought for food. In 1789 a loaf of bread cost an entire day's wages. Workers and farmers were starving. They rioted to protest the price of food. These riots were the first signs of revolution.

KING LOUIS XVI OF FRANCE says good-bye to his family before he is beheaded by the revolutionaries in 1793.

3 THEY WERE FEARED. The revolution terrified monarchs across Europe. They worried that they could end up beheaded too. In 1792 they formed an alliance and attacked the new French republic.

4 THEY LOST CONTROL. It wasn't long before the revolutionaries turned on one another. Rival groups accused each other of betraying the revolution. Thousands were arrested and charged with treason. From September 1793 to July 1794, up to 40,000 people were executed. That time became known as the Reign of Terror.

5 THEY LOST THEIR HEADS. Most of the revolution's victims were executed by guillotine. This was a tall wooden frame fitted with a heavy metal blade. The blade was raised with a rope—and then dropped on the victim's neck. The guillotine became a symbol of the revolutionaries' brutality.

NAPOLEON HAD A BAD TEMPER as a teenager, so his classmates called him a "Corsican savage" and said he belonged in a zoo.

2

One-Man Revolution

The general leads France to victory.

Napoleon Bonaparte had finally made himself the most powerful man in France. It was more than even he had dreamed possible. He had grown up on Corsica, an island that was bought by France just after he was born. At the military school he attended in France, his wealthy classmates made fun of his shabby clothes.

But he had shown them all. He had worked his way up through the army and proven his brilliance on the battlefield. And now he had won control of France itself.

NAPOLEON'S TROOPS DRAG their weapons and supplies over the snowy, treacherous Alps in May 1800.

Napoleon wasted no time in taking charge. He and his wife, Josephine, moved into the Tuileries Palace, where generations of French kings had lived. He imposed a new constitution on France. It allowed the First Consul to make all laws and appoint all government officials. Napoleon had made himself a king in everything but name. "I had been nourished by reflecting on liberty," he said, "but I thrust it aside when it obstructed my path."

Back to the Battlefield

Now it was time to return to the battlefield. France had been under siege by the kingdoms of Europe since 1792. One of these kingdoms, Austria, had sent an army toward the French border. Napoleon saw a chance to crush the Austrians and force them to make peace.

On May 15, 1800, Napoleon launched one of the most daring invasions the world has ever known. He marched his men over the towering Alps and into Italy. His soldiers took apart cannons and packed them into hollowed-out trees. They dragged the sledlike trees over snow-covered passes.

Pushed on by Napoleon, the army made the crossing

in just five days. They met the Austrians near the Italian town of Marengo. By midday, the Austrian commander had left the battlefield, certain that he had won. Just then, however, one of Napoleon's generals appeared with reinforcements. "This battle is completely lost," he told Napoleon. "But it is only two o'clock. There is time to win another."

Victory

Napoleon blasted the Austrian line with artillery. Then he finished them off with a cavalry charge. Within 24 hours, the Austrians had agreed to withdraw from Italy. Both Austria and Great Britain signed a peace treaty with France. For the first time in more than ten years, France was not fighting for its survival.

Once again there was a celebration. The grateful French citizens rewarded Napoleon by electing him "First Consul for Life." The vote was an astounding 3,568,885 to 8,374.

Few people had the courage to point out that Napoleon's new interior minister had supervised the counting.

Fixing France

Between wars, Napoleon launched an all-out effort to remake life in France.

"A new government must dazzle," Napoleon once said. He did more than dazzle. He changed France in ways that are still important. Here are a few examples.

EDUCATION. Napoleon developed a network of schools and colleges. He created thousands of scholarships for talented students.

INFRASTRUCTURE. He built canals and roads and improved sewer systems.

LAW. He created the Napoleonic Code, a new set of laws to govern France. For the first time, there were no special privileges for people with money or power. Many countries today base their laws on the Napoleonic Code.

3

Ruler of the World

A crown on his head, Napoleon sets out to battle all of Europe.

December 2, 1804, dawned cold and gray. It had snowed during the night. The cobblestone streets in the heart of Paris were slick with muddy slush. Inside Notre Dame Cathedral, Europe's most powerful leaders shivered in their silks and jewels. They had been waiting for Napoleon for hours.

It was unlike him to be late. But he had taken his time this morning. He wanted to enjoy every moment of the day. Finally Napoleon was bathed, perfumed, and draped in diamonds, silks, and fur. He pulled his brother Joseph in front of a mirror. "If only our father could see us now," he said.

Crowning Glory

Napoleon and Josephine pulled up to Notre Dame in a gold-and-crystal carriage. Napoleon strode into the cathedral. At the end of the carpeted aisle, Pope Pius VII waited to crown him emperor.

But Napoleon did not intend to receive the crown from anyone. Instead he grabbed the jeweled crown and set it firmly on his own head.

NAPOLEON PREPARES to place the imperial crown on Josephine's head as the pope looks on.

Then he crowned Josephine. With that act, the last traces of democracy disappeared in France. Napoleon had claimed the right to pass his crown on to his children just like the French kings of old.

Now Emperor Napoleon was free to pursue his true dream—the conquest of Europe. "I wanted to rule the world," he explained later. "And in order to do this I needed unlimited power."

In August 1805 the French army went on the move again. The kingdoms of Europe had formed another alliance against France. The Austrians were marching toward the Rhine River on the French border. Napoleon was determined to strike before they could invade. He drove his men day and night east toward the Rhine.

The French army crossed the river on September 25. The Austrian army fell back before Napoleon's relentless advance. By November Napoleon had seized the Austrian capital of Vienna. In December he caught up with the combined Austrian and Russian forces at a town called Austerlitz. More than 150,000 soldiers faced each other on a hilly battlefield.

NAPOLEON (in grey overcoat) and his men pull Russian soldiers out of a freezing lake after the Battle of Austerlitz. Thousands of Russians had fallen through the ice as they retreated.

The Battle of Austerlitz began in a cold morning mist. Napoleon had been awake all night planning his strategy. He deliberately weakened his right flank to lure the enemy into attacking there. The Russians and the Austrians took the bait and deserted the center of their line. "One sharp blow," Napoleon said, "and the war is over."

The French army burst through the fog. They attacked the center of the enemy line with a fury. By the afternoon, the battle was over. At least 23,000 men had been killed or wounded.

"Behold, a Hero!"

Napoleon congratulated his troops. "I will lead you back to France," he said. "My people will greet you with joy, and it will be enough for you to say, 'I was at the Battle of Austerlitz' for people to exclaim, 'Behold, a hero!'"

After the Battle of Austerlitz, Napoleon seemed unstoppable. Over the next two years he built an empire that extended across most of Europe. He was the most powerful man in the world—for now.

All in the Family

As Napoleon's empire grew, he had newly conquered states to rule. What better way to control them than to put a Bonaparte in charge? Here's a guide to the most powerful family in Europe in the early 1800s.

F R A N C E

S P A I N

JOSEPH (brother)
King of Naples (1806–1808)
and of Spain (1808–1813)

LOUIS (brother)
King of Holland

JEROME (brother)
King of Westphalia

EUGENE
(stepson)
Viceroy of Italy

PAULINE (sister)
Duchess of Guastalla

ELISA (sister)
Grand Duchess
of Tuscany

Rome

CAROLINE (sister)
Queen of Naples

NAPOLEON II
(son)
King of Rome

ITALY

**JOACHIM-NAPOLEON
MURAT** (brother-in-law)
King of Naples and Sicily

29

4

Downfall

At the height of his power, the emperor starts a fight he can't finish.

By 1811 Napoleon was under intense strain. He had been working 20-hour days for more than a decade. He was at the peak of his career, but there were signs of decline. He had a painful skin condition and chronic ulcers.

Also, Napoleon had become extremely suspicious. He used a vast network of spies to hunt down his political opponents. His secret police jailed dissenters and closed down newspapers that criticized him.

It was a lonely existence. "I like only those people who are useful to me," Napoleon said, "and then only so long as they are useful."

Challenging Russia

Worst of all for Napoleon, his empire was coming apart at the seams. The emperor had wanted to attack his archenemy, Great Britain. But Britain's navy was much stronger than France's, so Napoleon had no way to invade the island country. Napoleon had ordered the nations of Europe to boycott—stop trade with—Britain until the British surrendered. But resistance to the emperor's boycott was growing. Smugglers brought British goods into European ports. Rebels in Spain began killing French soldiers one by one.

Finally Russia announced it would resume trade with Britain. Napoleon responded the way he knew best. He assembled the largest army the world had ever known. In June 1812 he led 600,000 soldiers east toward Russia.

The biggest invasion in history turned into a grand disaster. The Russians retreated before the French advance. As they pulled back, they destroyed food supplies and poisoned wells. The massive French army slowly started to fall apart. Soldiers and their horses starved to death. Disease spread through the ranks.

The French finally reached Moscow on September 14. The Russian capital had been deserted. That night fires broke out, and most of Moscow burned to the ground.

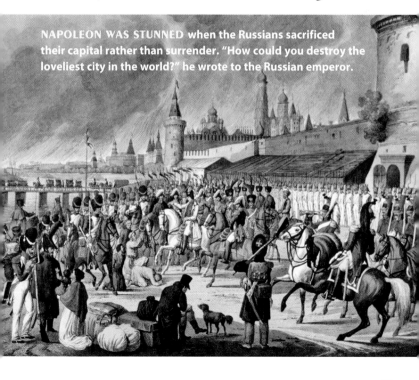

NAPOLEON WAS STUNNED when the Russians sacrificed their capital rather than surrender. "How could you destroy the loveliest city in the world?" he wrote to the Russian emperor.

The Russians had left Napoleon's army with nothing to conquer.

Napoleon's desperate soldiers lost faith in their leader. One-third of the French army had been destroyed. The survivors were starving, exhausted, and unwilling to march any farther into Russia.

MANY OF NAPOLEON'S MEN froze or starved to death during the disastrous retreat from Moscow.

Retreat, Surrender, and Exile

Napoleon had no choice but to order a retreat. His ragged army headed west, leaving cannons and wagons behind. In the end, five out of every six soldiers who had followed Napoleon into Russia did not return home.

The French empire would never be the same—and neither would its emperor. As Napoleon remarked on his return to Paris, "There is only one step from the sublime to the ridiculous."

Near the end of 1813, four European nations invaded France from the east. For a few months, Napoleon showed some of his old brilliance on the battlefield. But it was too late. His enemies were too powerful.

The emperor finally surrendered on April 11, 1814. The next morning he swallowed a vial of poison that he had worn around his neck for years. He broke into a sweat and began to vomit. But the poison had lost its strength. To Napoleon's disappointment, he survived.

The rulers of Europe exiled Napoleon to Elba, a small island near Corsica. Just a year earlier, Napoleon had reigned over half a continent. Now he ruled an obscure island with a population of less than 25,000.

NAPOLEON IS CARRIED into the Tuileries Palace on the shoulders of his cheering soldiers a month after he escaped from exile.

5

Waterloo

Napoleon makes his last stand on a battlefield in Belgium.

Napoleon tried to settle into life on Elba. He designed a new flag for the tiny island. He drew up plans to reform its economy and government. But the work held his attention for only nine months.

On the night of February 26, 1815, Napoleon assembled 700 men, seven ships, and four big guns. Silently, he sailed into the open sea. Three days later he landed on French soil with his tiny army.

As he and his men marched toward Paris, they were stopped by a battalion of King Louis XVIII's troops. Louis XVIII had become king of France after Napoleon was exiled. Napoleon approached the opposing force. He opened the front of his gray coat. "It is I, Napoleon," he shouted. "Kill your emperor if you wish."

No one moved, so Napoleon added an outright lie. "The wisest men in the Paris government have summoned me from Elba," he announced. "My return is backed by the three leading powers of Europe."

The king's men threw their hats in the air and cheered, "Long live the emperor!"

The Emperor Returns

Napoleon reached Paris in the spring. Thousands of supporters had joined his army. Crowds cheered his arrival and carried him into the royal palace. Louis XVIII fled.

Napoleon's second term as emperor began and ended as the first had—with war. By the time he reached Paris, his enemies had already begun to mobilize. Britain, Austria, Russia, and Prussia pledged a total of

600,000 troops. Napoleon's army numbered less than 300,000.

The two sides met near the Belgian town of Waterloo on June 17. The battle began at noon the next day. It ended at nightfall with the French running for their lives. Nearly 50,000 men lay dead on the battlefield.

Exiled, Again

This time the kings of Europe took no chances with Napoleon. They exiled him to the tiny volcanic island of St. Helena. He would spend the rest of his

NAPOLEON (left) at Waterloo. His disastrous defeat there marked the end of his spectacular and bloody career.

days in the South Atlantic Ocean, 700 miles from the nearest land. Thousands of men stood guard over the shoreline of his island prison.

Napoleon spent six cold, lonely years on St. Helena. His health grew worse, and he suffered from terrible stomach pains. Convinced that he was being poisoned by British agents, he stopped eating.

On May 5, 1821, at the age of 51, Napoleon died. With his final words, he called out for his true loves: "France . . . army . . . head of army . . . Josephine." ✂

NAPOLEON SPENT his final six years on St. Helena.

Word Games

Napoleon made his mark on the world—and on the way we speak. Here's a brief glossary of phrases the emperor left behind.

Napoleon complex: This term describes someone who feels insecure about being short and makes up for it by being overly aggressive and ambitious. But Napoleon was actually of average height. Historians might not have thought to convert his height in French inches to the smaller English inches.

To meet one's Waterloo: This phrase comes from Napoleon's final battle. It's used when someone comes face-to-face with the ultimate challenge—and loses.

A picture is worth a thousand words: Some people claim that Napoleon coined this phrase. What he actually said (in French) was: "A good sketch is better than a long speech." Close enough?

An Extraordinary Man?

According to this speech, which Napoleon made to his doctor on St. Helena, the former emperor never lost confidence in himself.

as one of the bloodiest tyrants in history

In spite of all the libels, I have no fear whatever about my fame. Posterity will do me justice. The truth will be known; and the good I have done will be compared with the faults I have committed. I am not uneasy as to the result. Had I succeeded, I would have died with the reputation of the greatest man that ever existed. As it is, although I have failed, I shall be considered as an extraordinary man: my elevation was unparalleled, because unaccompanied by crime. I have fought 50 pitched battles, almost all of which I have won. I have framed and carried into effect a code of laws that will bear my name to the most distant posterity. I raised myself from nothing to be the most powerful monarch in the world. Europe was at my feet. I have always been of the opinion that the sovereignty lay in the people. In fact, the imperial government was a kind of republic. Called to the head of it by the voice of the nation, my maxim was, *la carrière est ouverte aux talens* [careers are open to talent] without distinction of birth or fortune.

Not that I ever did anything wrong!

Unless you think overthrowing the government twice is a crime.

Waterloo was a fluke!

You'll buy that, right?

Timeline: Napoleon

1778: Napoleon wins a scholarship to a military school in France.

1796: Napoleon marries Josephine de Beauharnais. Then he leads an army to victory during his first campaign against Austria in Italy.

1804: Napoleon passes his Napoleonic Code and crowns himself emperor of France.

| 1769 | 1778 | 1793 | 1796 | 1799 | 1804 | 180 |

1769: Napoleon Bonaparte is born in Corsica.

1799: Napoleon returns from Egypt and seizes power in France.

1805: The French army defeats Russia and Austria at the Battle of Austerlitz.

1793: In the middle of the French Revolution, Napoleon wins fame by defeating soldiers loyal to King Louis XVI at Toulon.

Bonaparte

1810: Because Josephine is unable to produce an heir, Napoleon divorces her and marries Marie-Louise, daughter of the Austrian emperor.

1815: Napoleon returns to power, loses the Battle of Waterloo, and is exiled to St. Helena.

1811: Marie-Louise gives birth to a son, Napoleon II.

1814: Napoleon is exiled to Elba.

806 1810 1811 1812 1813 1814 1815 1821

1806: Napoleon defeats Prussia at the battles of Jena and Auerstedt.

1812: Napoleon launches his disastrous invasion of Russia.

1813: The French are defeated at the Battle of the Nations by troops from Austria, Prussia, Russia, and Sweden.

1821: Napoleon dies on St. Helena.

45

RESOURCES

Here's a selection of books and websites for more information about Napoleon Bonaparte.

What to Read Next

NONFICTION

Arnold, James R. *The Aftermath of the French Revolution* (Aftermath of History). Minneapolis: Twenty-First Century Books, 2009.

Greenblatt, Miriam. *Napoleon Bonaparte and Imperial France* (Rulers and Their Times). New York: Marshall Cavendish Benchmark Books, 2006.

Heuston, Kimberley. *Napoleon: Emperor and Conqueror* (A Wicked History). New York: Franklin Watts, 2010.

Obstfeld, Raymond, ed. *Napoleon Bonaparte* (People Who Made History). San Diego: Greenhaven Press, 2001.

Streissguth, Thomas. *The Napoleonic Wars: Defeat of the Grand Army*. San Diego: Lucent Books, 2003.

FICTION

Broome, Errol. *Gracie and the Emperor*. Toronto: Annick Press, 2005.

Woodruff, Elvira. *Dear Napoleon, I Know You're Dead, But …* New York: Holiday House, 1992.

Websites

Liberty, Equality, Fraternity
http://chnm.gmu.edu/ revolution
This comprehensive site includes real letters and documents from the French Revolution, as well as images, maps, and even songs.

Napoleon
www.pbs.org/empires/ napoleon
This online companion to the PBS special *Napoleon* includes a timeline, mini-biographies, and an interactive simulator of the Battle of Waterloo.

Napoleon.org
www.napoleon.org/en/kids/ index.asp
The educational page of the Fondation Napoléon, an organization committed to the study of Napoleon and his family. Includes a family tree, timelines, and maps.

ALLIANCE (uh-LYE-uhnss) *noun* an agreement to work together

ARCHENEMY (arch-EN-uh-mee) *noun* the worst enemy

ARTILLERY (ar-TIL-uh-ree) *noun* large, powerful guns, such as cannons

BATTALION (buh-TAL-yun) *noun* in Napoleon's armies, a unit of about 840 soldiers

CAMPAIGN (kam-PAYN) *noun* a series of military actions in pursuit of a particular goal

CAVALRY (KAV-uhl-ree) *noun* soldiers who fight on horseback

CONQUEST (KON-kwest) *noun* something that is won, such as land or treasure

CONSTITUTION (kon-stuh-TOO-shuhn) *noun* the system of laws in a country that state the rights of the people and the powers of the government

CONSUL (KON-suhl) *noun* one of the three chief executives of France from 1799 to 1804; Napoleon was First Consul, the most powerful of the three

DISSENTER (di-SENT-uhr) *noun* one who disagrees with an idea or opinion

EXILE (EG-zile) *noun* the state of being cast out from one's homeland

FLANK (FLANGK) *noun* the far left or right side of a line of soldiers

LEGISLATURE (LEJ-iss-lay-chur) *noun* a group of people who have the power to make or change the laws of a country or state

MAXIM (MAK-sim) *noun* a short statement that expresses a general truth

MONARCH (MON-ark) *noun* a ruler who inherits his or her position

POSTERITY (pah-STEHR-ih-tee) *noun* future generations

REPUBLIC (ri-PUB-lik) *noun* a form of government in which citizens elect representatives to run the government

REVOLUTION (rev-uh-LOO-shuhn) *noun* an uprising by the people that changes their country's system of government

SOVEREIGNTY (SOV-ruhn-tee) *noun* supreme power or authority

TREASON (TREE-zuhn) *noun* the crime of betraying one's country

ULCER (UHL-sur) *noun* an open, painful sore

INDEX

METRIC CONVERSIONS

Feet to meters: 1 ft is about 0.3 m
Miles to kilometers: 1 mi is about 1.6 km
Pounds to kilograms: 1 lb is about 0.45 kg